ISBN – 978-0-9917887-5-0

I0105501

This book is dedicated to my beloved dad, Thomas who by his excellent example taught us the importance of honesty and integrity.

Special thanks to Angel Brkic whose artistic talents brought these words to life.
I am so grateful for the love and support of my dear husband Barry, and all my family and friends that encouraged me on the way.

Matlox Publishing

When Lizzy wakes up, the very first thing she says is "I am going to have an amazing day today!" and then she would list all the things she was thankful for in her life. Lizzy did this every morning.

When Lizzy was at school she passed a boy in the hall and smiled at him and said,"Hi Tommy"

Tommy just kept walking and looking at the floor, so Lizzy went to him and asked, "What is wrong? You look so tired and sad."

Tommy kept his head down as he mumbled, "I don't know what's wrong but I do feel tired and sad." "Hmmm," said Lizzy. "Why don't you tell me what you are thinking about."

Tommy thought about the question Lizzy had asked him and then he said "a boy in my class called me stupid today, I am not very good at sports, and I really don't like how I look."

"Oh" said Lizzy, "I know why you are tired and sad." "You do?" said Tommy.

"Yes Tommy, It is those thoughts you are thinking. They are making you sad, but I can help you change those thoughts just like that" said Lizzy, as she snapped her fingers. "Come to my house after school and I will help you," Lizzy said.

Tommy came to Lizzy's house and he was looking very sad, Tommy said, "Do you really think you can help me feel happy?"

Lizzy picked up a mirror that was lying on a table and said "Look into this mirror and right into your own eyes and say "I love you."
Tommy took the mirror and almost in a whisper said "I love you." Lizzy said "say it like you mean it Tommy," so he said it louder and on the third "I love you," Tommy started to smile, and said, "that does make me feel better."

Lizzy said "next I want you to think of the things you are thankful for in your life." Tommy said "There are so many things I am thankful for in my life. I am thankful for my family, my toys, my clothes and my friends, and especially you, Lizzy."

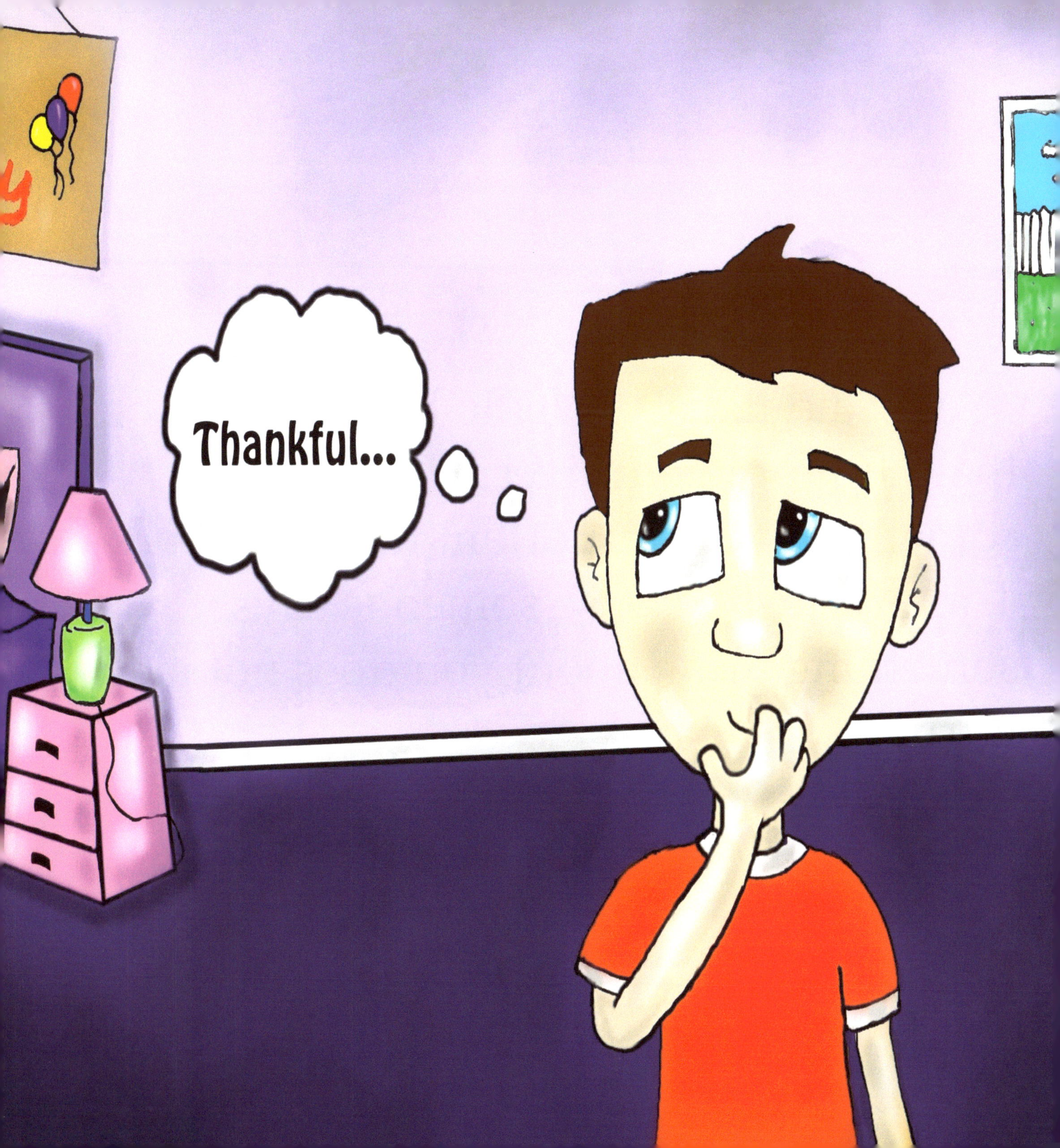
Thankful...

"Yes," said Lizzy. "We do have a lot to be thankful for in our lives. Here is something very important to remember, Tommy, just because someone says something mean about you does not make it true."

Tommy thought for a minute and said "You are right about that, thank you Lizzy. I feel so much happier."

Lizzy and Tommy walked downstairs into the kitchen. There were a lot of magazines and some scissors on the table. Lizzy told Tommy to look through the magazines and find words like love, joy, believe, laugh, and dream, and cut them out to paste on a piece of cardboard. "We will call these our happy words," Lizzy said.

When all the words were pasted, they stapled a string on the back of the cardboard. Lizzy said "Hang this near your bed so that these words will be the first thing you see when you wake up." Tommy liked that idea. There were so many happy words to see.

After playing for a while Tommy said "I have to go home now" and as he was walking away, he said, "I will pay it forward." Lizzy asked "What do you mean?" Tommy said "I am going to help someone else change the thoughts that are making them sad so they can be happy too. I am thankful you did that for me, Lizzy."

"That's a great idea," Lizzy shouted "Pay it forward, Tommy". "Lizzy stood at the door and waved goodbye to Tommy. She yelled as loud as she could to him. "This has been an amazing day!"

www.ingramcontent.com/pod-product-compliance
Lightning Source LLC
Chambersburg PA
CBHW040231070426
42447CB00030B/153